WI
HOUSE

Come Under Her Seven Pillars

JOHN W. WALLACE

ww.BurkhartBooks.com

Bedford, Texas

DEDICATION

This book is dedicated to the wisest woman I know, my wife Suzanne. I have learned wisdom from watching her live her life before God and others. I have been challenged by her example and sometimes by her loving rebukes. I have seen the effect of her words of wisdom in helping transform others' lives. It is no surprise to me that Wisdom is personified in Proverbs as a woman. I can see her in Suzanne's eyes. I love you dearly, even more than the almost-fifty-years-ago day of our wedding! Our Lord has graciously invested so much in you, and you are bringing such a return on that investment. Thank you for being such a huge part of my life and letting me be a part of yours.

ACKNOWLEDGEMENTS

So many people have contributed to my life and the portion of wisdom I have the responsibility to carry. I've learned from parents, teachers, and coaches about life - what works really well and what doesn't work at all.

As I've put forth in this book, I first acknowledge the triune God—Father, Son, and Holy Spirit and their work in my life to teach, train, rebuke, correct, and encourage me. They have used the voice of the Scriptures and the voice of the Spirit through hearing in my spirit and through hearing from other wise sons and daughters of the High King.

Again, as I have acknowledged in another book, I thank those who have mentored me through the years: Sam Owen, Steve Atkinson, John Wimber, Jim Hyton, Bill Johnson, Ben Fike, and Jack Taylor. These men, along with several of my brothers and sisters in Christ, have mentored me through books, conferences, videos, phone calls, and personal one-on-one conversations. They have answered many of my questions, prayed me through situations often difficult and confusing, and have proved to be role models of people walking in wisdom. They have entered Wisdom's House and beckoned me to follow them. Grace and peace to them all.

CONTENTS

FOREWORD

The book you have opened is filled with thoughts from the mind of God. John Wallace has devoted most of His life to hearing God speak to him, learning from others who were hearing God, and experiencing the affirming validation of God's shared mind and wisdom as his most valued life treasure. One of the most obvious qualities of wisdom guiding the thinking person is the adaptation to a better way to think, to relate to themselves and others, and to inspire others to experience the same wisdom. The secular world knows this concept as "early adoption," as described by Everett Rogers in Diffusion of Innovations. A person adopting new products in technology is an "early adopter." Five categories of advancement or lack thereof are identified: innovators, early adopters, the early majority, the late majority, and the laggards.

I have known and admired John Wallace from the epic years of spiritual awakening starting in the 1980s. Our friendship grew out of our mutual friendship with John Wimber, an innovator who was an early adopter. John Wallace had already made a significant change in his professional career. He was in the early stages of what would have been an illustrious career in dentistry when the change occurred. Obtaining a doctorate in dentistry and a very successful start in an office in the North Dallas area is no small achievement. But a call resonated in him to know more about God, which led to his commitment to pursue a study of theology at Dallas Theological Seminary. Dentistry by day would pay the bills to enable him to study about God on a part-time basis.

The urgency of the call was such that he found long hours limiting the qualities of his studies about

God conflicted by his day job as a dentist. Adopting or adapting to a better way followed. He left dentistry to study full time. After this transition, he was not studying about God as much as studying with God. Thinking with God was becoming part of his life experience. As that successful phase was completed with a degree in theology, he began experiencing the presence of God in new ways. God was present—loving him and loving others through him. From the life and ministry of John Wimber, he saw "Christ in you" modeled by Wimber, which led to knowing people's needs and meeting them both supernaturally and practically. Information that he had gained about God was changing by knowing God's thoughts through words of knowledge. Knowing God, knowing as you are known, and knowing others as God knows them became the essence of the life and ministry of John Wallace. With a brilliant mind that could obtain a doctorate in dentistry and a Master of Theology degree, he was embracing wisdom beyond the reaches of mere intellectual comprehension. Instead of a conventional approach to church planting and church life, he allowed the mind of Christ to guide him to people of every kind of need and background. Many of people were impoverished and in bondage to addictions of every kind. Instead of ministry among the suburban successful, he made his way into Deep Ellum among the broken-hearted, needing restoration. You will read his own account of his experience of learning to think with God in the House of Wisdom as defined in this significant book.

It is my studied opinion, meaning I have carefully considered, that John is still a dentist—a dentist repairing spiritual teeth so we can bite off the delicious fruit God gives us and then chew each mouth full so that the full measure of nourishment is realized. More than that, because our spiritual teeth are healthy, we can chew the food for thought into small pieces and get all the taste God supplies in His thoughts. Our mouths will be filled with the delicious experience that our spiritual taste buds crave—tasting and seeing that God is good. As Eugene Peterson worded it in The Message; "Open your mouth and taste, open your eyes and see—how good God is. Blessed are you who run to him" (Psa. 34:8).

Books contain two primary disclosures: the message and the messenger. A message resonating with life and reality can only exist because the messenger is sharing words and thoughts that reveal God's thoughts shared with them. Knowing God, not knowing information about God, has been the primary pursuit of this author for some forty-plus years. John is a scholar, a teacher who remained a student-teacher across these four decades. He is enriched by knowing word meanings and connotations with better applications, but in John's scale of values, they are secondary to knowing God's presence and God's shared thoughts.

In a long-ago time of world history with similar parallels to our world today, God made an astonishing offer to an amazing man. He said, "Come let's reason together." Isaiah accepted the offer, and with it, God's way of thinking. God's own wisdom resulted in the mindfulness of a messenger of God. Empty minds that could not distinguish good from evil, light from darkness, and sweetness from bitter were filled with self-serving wisdom created from their own clever shrewdness, which was the opposite of what God thought. God's messenger, Isaiah, learned to receive and share the mind of God in what is often called the Gospel of Isaiah. This gospel, like the four gospels written 700 years later, was the "good news of God's son, sharing with us God's forgiveness, God's thoughts, and God's way."

Isaiah experienced God Himself. He saw Him; He felt Him: He heard Him, and He shared Him with us in his writings. He describes experiencing God - seeing God exalted in reigning glory that covers the whole earth. A transformed messenger wrote a transforming message. Isaiah could not change himself, so God took a live coal from the altar and transformed a man who saw himself unclean, unworthy, and "undone." Isaiah was transformed into a man cleansed, commissioned, and capable of enjoying the glory of God he has seen covering the earth. God's shared glory became part of him.

This book contains the same emphasis. John Wallace does not make the many facets of God's wisdom a commodity or benefit that can be obtained without a relationship with God. John wants us to know God as Immanuel, God with us, so we can see God, know God, and enjoy His shared joy. The doctor of spiritual dentistry wants us to taste the love of God, the joy of God, and the value God has for all people, even those we count as our enemies. Those we may think are our enemies, God knows as His neighbors, His children living away from home who are welcomed back the moment they open their mouth to take and taste His life as their own.

Profound is the best word to describe this book that my mind furnished from its word search in my neurological files. Having accepted that word as a good choice, I decided to look at dictionary meanings and found a long list of synonyms verifying that profound as a good description of what you are about to read. I found authentic, classic, genuine, real, constant, endless, eternal, perpetual, undying, to name less than half the list.

An exaggeration, though unintended, on my part by using this word would not fit the integrity of the book nor the character of the author. Profound's meanings of authentic, genuine, real, and constant describe John Wallace as a person. The shades of meaning in the words classic, endless, eternal, perpetual, and undying give measurements of the depth of this book's message revealing Wisdom as part of God's own nature and character. John's careful treatment of the eternal thoughts of God, provided to us from God's incarnational life in Christ, offers us a mind we can access. The shared life and mind of Christ is a profound characteristic of this entire book. The eternal one came to us in time so that in Him, eternal life starts now in us. Eternal life shared with us in Christ gives us an "eternal kind of life" -here, now - as Dallas Willard declared. Our minds are meant to be interactive with both heaven and earth, eternity, and time. Jesus made it very clear that we will think forever. God's will, being done on earth in the way it is being done in heaven, is impossible unless the mind of Christ becomes part of our mind. Instead of our own attempt at will power, the mind of Christ releases love's attending power, and our minds and will experience love's power. Our will power is weak and undependable, but God's way of loving empowers our will, restores our mind, and guides us into God's way of thinking and living. The power of the gospel is the power of God's love released in us through the mind of Christ. Our mind is renewed by embracing God's thoughts, which leads to enjoying His ways.

God's offer is to share His ingenious loving mind's supply of life-giving thoughts. That is the offer of this book, that is like no other I have read. Carefully consider His offer that follows for you. As you read this book, you will find God's own thoughts becoming your thoughts and God's ways becoming your ways.

Jim Hylton
Pastor, Author, Conference Speaker
Ft. Worth, Texas

INTRODUCTION

Then the king said, "Give the first woman the living child, and by no means kill him. She is his mother." When all Israel heard of the judgment which the king had handed down, they feared the king, for they saw that the wisdom of God was in him to administer justice. (1 Kings 3:27–28, NAS)

Perhaps you've read the story. King Solomon, early in his reign, asked God for wisdom (we'll get to that prayer). Soon that wisdom was required. Two women presented themselves before him; each one was saying that the baby with them is her child. Solomon's decision is a sword to sever the babe in half and give each woman half! One woman protests, preferring that the other woman have the whole child and, thus, revealing herself as the true mother and preserving her son's life. As a result of the execution of Solomon's decision, note the response: "ALL Israel heard … feared … saw that the wisdom of God was in him …."

I think most people would say they'd love to exhibit some of the wisdom Solomon exercised. It's even become a saying—"the wisdom of Solomon." This kind of wisdom demonstrated the presence of God! Wouldn't you like to know that you are a person in whom others see the wisdom of God? We read of the same effect his wisdom had on the Queen of Sheba (1 Kings 10:6-9): "How blessed are your men, how blessed are these your servants who stand before you continually and hear your wisdom" (verse 8).

Is this wisdom accessible for us today? If so, how do we get it? How does it work? I offer my insights in this book because I'm convinced we ARE carriers of a wisdom greater than Solomon's. My intention is to guide us on this journey of exploring the wisdom God has provided for us.

It seems terribly audacious for any human to write on wisdom. People write about that in which they have expertise or some familiarity. Let me emphatically state that I have no expertise in wisdom. But some people write about what they love. And I love wisdom. I realize that writing on a non-fiction topic, an author might portray themselves as an authority, as an expert on the subject. Just as I just wrote, I, by no stretch of what is true or what is imagined, present myself as a "wisdom expert." I consider the wisdom I have gained, which is a fraction of a fraction of the totality of wisdom, has accumulated through God's grace and through many years of following Jesus. In His Word, the Scriptures are found wisdom. His Spirit is the "spirit of wisdom" (Is. 11:2) and, most important, as we'll see in Chapter 1, wisdom is found in Jesus Himself.

I have the privilege of meeting regularly with "Incendiaries"—burning, passionate, Jesus-loving, younger leaders in different walks of life. I share my life with them- my victories and defeats, my sorrows and joys, my regrets and celebrations, prophecies, and prayers. I tell them, early on in our relationship, that wisdom is acquired two ways, and one way hurts more than the other! I've gained a good deal of the wisdom that I have by the latter method! So, as I examine this dynamic gift of God, know that much of the wisdom I have or can communicate to you has been the hard-fought, painfully-acquired kind which was gained, many times, by the mistakes and failures that I've experienced.

Proverbs 9:1-4 proclaims to us:

> *¹Wisdom has built her house,*
> *She has hewn out her seven pillars;*
> *²She has prepared her food, she has mixed*
> *her wine; she has also set her table;*
> *³She has sent out her maidens, she calls*
> *From the tops of the heights of the city:*
> *⁴"Whoever is naive, let him turn in here!"*

In the book of Proverbs, three types of people are addressed, over and over: the naive (sometimes translated "simple"), the fool, and the wise. The wise person is one who is learning God's ways and applying them to their lives; the fool is the person who knows God's ways and disregards them; the naive or simple person is the one who has not yet learned His ways or is just learning them. In these verses of Proverbs 9, Wisdom is extending an invitation to the naive, to those who are ready and willing to learn from her. If we are willing, we're invited into her house. Notice what kind of house it is. Read, again, verse one: "Wisdom has built her house, she has hewn out (cut or prepared) her seven pillars." There are seven "columns" upon which Wisdom's house is supported.

Scholars have given us various interpretations of what these "seven pillars" represent:

- "This hewing out of pillars suggests the splendor of the completed building" (Lange and Zockler, *The Proverbs of Solomon*).

-

- "What seems certain is that the house described here represents an image of luxury and, from the widespread use of seven as a perfect number, a complete and ideal or perfect building." (Rayburn, *A Handbook On Proverbs*)

- "The significance of 'seven" is not elucidated, … but a more reasonable explanation is that it refers to the seven days of creation (note Wisdom's role in creation in 8:22–31)."

- "The number seven generally denotes perfection; it is the covenant number, expressive of harmony and unity generally, the signature of holiness and blessing, completeness and rest." (Spence, *The Pulpit Commentary: Proverbs*)

Although I see value in some of these explanations, I believe there is a more practical and more applicable meaning to the number "seven." As I have studied the book of Proverbs, I have seen the repeated use of seven terms to describe aspects of wisdom:

1) KNOWLEDGE
2) UNDERSTANDING
3) COUNSEL
4) PRUDENCE
5) DISCERNMENT
6) DISCRETION
7) INSTRUCTION

Each is a different Hebrew word. Each has its own particular, rich portrayal of the wisdom of God. Each one provides support for Wisdom's house. As we begin to operate, from time to time, in all seven of these aspects of wisdom, we enjoy the "fullness" of wisdom. It is in these terms, taken together, I see the "splendor" and the "perfection" and the" holiness, completeness and rest" of wisdom as the authors state above.

So let's take a journey through these seven Hebrew terms. Two of my friends are Jewish believers in Yeshua (Jesus). Over the past years, they have helped me to appreciate the richness of both Hebrew words and even the Hebrew letters that compose the words. I have a love for God's word, and these tutors have given me even more to love and more in which to be fascinated. Going further than the precious meanings of the words, I'm going to give examples of their use in my life and the lives of my family and friends. I'll challenge you to put them into practice.

Solomon's dad, King David, told him, "The beginning of wisdom is: Acquire wisdom; and with all your acquiring, get understanding." (Proverbs 4:7). You don't go after or seek to acquire something in which you see no value. To access the full measure of wisdom's "house," we need to see it as valuable to us in order for us to have a desire to acquire it.

Acquiring and walking in wisdom IS valuable. As we will see, the Scriptures tell us that it is fully living to have wisdom and exercise it. Acquiring and walking is a journey, a process, a path that we walk down all of our days.

Ready for the journey into Wisdom's House? Any building structure is only as strong as its foundation. So let's start by appreciating what wisdom is built upon in Chapter One.

THE FOUNDATION OF WISDOM'S HOUSE

To those of us who have believed in Jesus, we know that we have His life within us:

> *To whom God willed to make known what is the riches of the glory of this mystery among the Gentiles, which is* **Christ in you**, *the hope of glory.*
> Colossians 1:27

> *I have been crucified with Christ; and it is no longer I who live, but* **Christ lives in me***; and the life which I now live in the flesh I live by faith of the Son of God, who loved me and gave Himself up for me.*
> Galatians 2:20

> *Always carrying about in the body the dying of Jesus, so that the* **life of Jesus** *also may be manifested in our body. For we who live are constantly being delivered over to death for Jesus' sake, so that the* **life of Jesus** *also may be manifested in our mortal flesh.*
> 2 Corinthians 4:10–11

Who is this Jesus who lives within us?

> *… that their hearts may be encouraged, having been knit together in love, and attaining to all the wealth that comes from the full assurance of understanding,*

> *resulting in a true knowledge of God's mystery, that
> is,* **Christ Himself in whom are hidden all the
> treasures of wisdom and knowledge**.
> Colossians 2:2–3

This Jesus that lives within us, holds all of the treasures of wisdom and knowledge! This Jesus lives in you if you've accepted what He's done for you, and you've given your life to Him! This same Jesus, in you, is the endless resource for the wisdom of God!

Not only do you have within you the wisdom Solomon had, but you also have something greater!

"The Queen of the South will rise up with the men of this generation at the judgment and condemn them, because she came from the ends of the earth to hear the wisdom of Solomon; and behold, *something greater* than Solomon is here." (Luke 11:31). Jesus was, of course, referring to Himself.

Our triune God—Father, Son, and Holy Spirit—is the Source and Supplier of wisdom. That's why in the apostle Paul's prayers, he makes requests for wisdom:

> *That the God of our Lord Jesus Christ, the Father
> of glory, may give to you a* **spirit of wisdom** *and of
> revelation in the knowledge of Him.*
> Ephesians 1:17

> *For this reason also, since the day we heard of it,
> we have not ceased to pray for you and to ask that
> you may be filled with the knowledge of His will
> in all* **spiritual wisdom** *and understanding ....*
> Colossians 1:9

And James:

> *But if any of you lacks **wisdom**, let him ask of God,*
> *who gives to all generously and without reproach,*
> *and it will be given to him.*
>
> James 1:5

Wisdom is one huge benefit of being a child of God! The One Who is wise lives within us. The "only wise God" (Rom. 16:19) offers us this wisdom. We need but ask.

In addition, the Holy Spirit is given to all who believe in Him. You cannot be a Christian, cannot be a child of God, without the Holy Spirit living within you -

> *However, you are not in the flesh but in the Spirit,*
> *if indeed the Spirit of God dwells in you. **But if***
> ***anyone does not have the Spirit of Christ, he does***
> ***not belong to Him**.*
>
> Romans 8:9

If we also have the Holy Spirit, again, I ask, who is this Holy Spirit? He is the Presence of Jesus—"the Spirit of Christ." Over 600 years before the birth of Jesus, the prophet Isaiah predicted the appearance of the Messiah, the Savior. Of Him, it is written:

> *The Spirit of the Lord will rest on Him,*
> *The **spirit of wisdom** and understanding,*
> *The spirit of counsel and strength,*
> *The spirit of knowledge and the fear of the Lord.*
>
> Isaiah 11:2

When Jesus came and taught in His hometown synagogue, notice the response of the people:

> *He came to His hometown and began teaching them*
> *in their synagogue, so that they were astonished,*
> *and said,* **"Where did this man get this wisdom**
> **and these miraculous powers?"**
>
> Matt. 13:54

The prophecy of Isaiah was fulfilled and being demonstrated in their midst!

Putting all this together, we can ask our Father God (the all-wise God) for wisdom. We have Jesus (Who "became to us wisdom from God ...." 1 Cor. 1:30), and we have the indwelling Holy Spirit (Who is the Spirit of wisdom). Every expression of God, all of the Trinity, is present to give us wisdom.

Back to Proverbs 9:1, which I referred to in the Introduction: "Wisdom has built her house; she has hewn her seven pillars." We will talk about the seven pillars which comprise the structure of Wisdom's house. But pillars must rest upon something. They must rest upon a foundation, a firm foundation. That foundation is the Lord Jesus:

> *For no man can lay a foundation other than the one*
> *which is laid, which is Jesus Christ.*
>
> 1 Cor. 3:11

This is where we begin walking in wisdom. A wise person is the one who is on a path, a journey toward a more intimate relationship with our Lord: Father, Son, and Holy Spirit. A person journeying on "the Path of the Wise" is journeying WITH the Father, Son, and Holy

Spirit. Imagine taking a road trip with the wisest Person in the universe. All along the way, you can converse with Him, ask Him questions, and listen as He tells you directions along the journey, perhaps giving you course corrections and pointing out the beautiful scenery—even parts of the scenery you would have missed because you just wanted to get to your destination. We walk this path with this One!

I often ask, during the day, for God's wisdom—for example, where and when to drive places and what routes to take. I ask Him for wisdom in decisions, great and small. I can tell you that when I haven't asked Him, when I've relied upon my own "savvy," it hasn't worked out so well! Again James (his name was really Jacob!) tells us that all we need to do if we lack wisdom is to ask. Have you ever tried saying, "Jesus, what do You think about this situation or this person?"

The foundation of the house of wisdom is Jesus. We must have Jesus living in us to exercise the wisdom of God. Jesus really does know you. Jesus really does love you. Jesus really does want to talk to you and listen as you talk to Him: worshipping Him, loving Him, telling Him how you feel, asking for His wisdom. In and through this interaction, you will see His glory, His infinite worth, and beauty. This is a relationship, and a relationship takes time and lots of communication. Please give it to Him as you walk out the journey!

Jesus is the foundation of Wisdom's house. Remember, as we look at each of the seven pillars of Wisdom's House that each pillar rests upon this foundation of Jesus. He is also the close companion on the path of those who are wise. Let's explore this relationship and interaction with our Lord in the next chapter as we look at some of the things the Scriptures characterize as wisdom.

Have I accepted Jesus? Have I given my life to the One Who loves me so and have received, in exchange, His life for me?

Do I see Jesus as the Source for any wisdom I desire or have?

Do I believe the Holy Spirit, the Spirit of wisdom, resides in me?

Do I continually ask Him for wisdom and listen or watch for His answer to my prayer?

CHAPTER 2

WHAT IS WISDOM?

Wh12at is wisdom anyway? When we say (or hear someone say), "That person is wise" what do we mean? What do we see in that person, or what is it that they said that caused us to categorize them as "wise?"

Much can be gained by seeing what the Scriptures say is wise and who the Scriptures say is wise:

WISDOM IS KNOWING AND PERFORMING A SKILL.

In both the construction of the tabernacle in the wilderness and in the construction of Solomon's temple, we are told that wisdom was given to individuals (for the tabernacle: Bezalel, Exodus 28:3; 31:3; 35:3; and for the temple: Hiram, 1 Kings 7:14) to perform the tasks of constructing these structures.

What can we gather from this? Wise living is to skillfully perform what you and I have been gifted and talented to do. NOTE: particularly in Bezalel's case, this skill is given by the Spirit of the Lord. In fact, this is the first instance of anyone in the Bible having the Holy Spirit, enabling him to artistically oversee and assemble the various items of the Lord's "tent of meeting." The Holy Spirit invested wisdom in an artist—I love it!

To respond to the Holy Spirit's moving in my life and to the promptings of the Spirit through others is wisdom. A friend of mine, years ago, was in a profession that no longer brought him joy or the satisfaction from the Lord that he had had previously. So he asked the Lord for a creative idea, some way that he could use a skill set (or be given a new skill set) that he could creatively move in. I don't know how much time went by, but one night in a dream, the Lord gave him an idea and a way to perform an artistic task. He saw this in a dream. He woke up, started to put it into practice, and it started a whole new chapter in his life, a way to joy and a way to support himself financially. God gave this man a heaven-sent creative idea and how to work it out artistically. That's wisdom!

WISDOM IS KNOWING AND FOLLOWING GOD'S STATUTES AND JUDGMENTS

See, I have taught you statutes and judgments just as the LORD my God commanded me that you should do thus in the land where you are entering to possess it. **So keep and do them, for that is your wisdom and your understanding** *in the sight of the peoples who will hear all these statutes and say, "Surely this great nation is* **a wise and understanding** *people."*

Dt 4:5–6

If God is all-wise (Rom. 16:27) and He is the one who created life and created life in us, then He knows how life ought to be best-lived. A creator of something is the one who knows how it works. When God gives laws, statutes, judgments, and commandments, these are not to punish us but to protect us. These are not to restrict us but to allow us to fully express life in the way we were created to express it.

And He [Jesus] *said to him, "YOU SHALL LOVE THE LORD YOUR GOD WITH ALL YOUR*

*HEART, AND WITH ALL YOUR SOUL, AND
WITH ALL YOUR MIND: This is the great
and foremost commandment. The second is like it,
YOU SHALL LOVE YOUR NEIGHBOR AS
YOURSELF. On these two commandments depend
the whole Law and the Prophets."*

Mt 22:37–40

*A new commandment I give to you that you love one
another, even as I have loved you,
that you also love one another.*

Jn 13:34

*He who has My commandments and keeps them is
the one who loves Me; and he who loves Me will be
loved by My Father, and I will love him and will
disclose Myself to him.*

Notice how Jesus tied keeping His commandments to love, to relationship. We are to follow His commands because we love Him and because we believe He loves us, not just to "keep the rules." The Passion Translation of this verse 21 starts out: "Loving me empowers you to obey my word." And notice the reward for lovingly obeying His commandments: "he who loves Me will be loved by My Father, and I will love him and will disclose Myself to him." Wow! A back-and-forth loving dynamic in our lives is promised with the additional bonus of increasing "disclosure" of Jesus to us. We step into further and deeper revelational and relational knowledge of our Lord!

Several decades ago, I had a very hard time forgiving someone who repeatedly hurt me. I knew what Jesus said about forgiveness:

*Then Peter came and said to Him, "Lord, how often
shall my brother sin against me and I forgive him?
Up to seven times?" Jesus *said to him, "I do not say
to you, up to seven times, but up to seventy times
seven.*

Matthew 18: 21,22

Up to that point, forgiving that person was difficult. I
was focused on the hurt caused by what the other person
had said to me, over and over again. Yet, I came to see
my disobedience to God's "statute" about forgiveness was
poisoning me, keeping me distant from God and from
that person. One of the wisest things I ever did was to
repent and follow God and take hold of His grace to
forgive that person. Wisdom was to follow God's loving
command to me. That's wisdom!

WISDOM IS KNOWING AND APPRECIATING
THE BREVITY OF LIFE

*So teach us to number our days,
That we may present to You a heart of wisdom.*

Ps 90:12

The authorship of Psalm 90 is attributed to Moses.
Think about it: Moses was witnessing people dying in
the desert as a result of God's judgment against their
unbelief. By some estimates, he was watching 102 people
per day being buried in the sand during those years
of wandering! Death was a daily companion. As he
witnessed this, he said, "Teach us to number our days …."

In another Psalm, David wrote:

As for man, his days are like grass;
As a flower of the field, so he flourishes.
When the wind has passed over it, it is no more,
And its place acknowledges it no longer.

Ps 103:15–16

When I was in my teens and twenties, the "shortness" of life seemed a distant fact that I didn't have to give much attention to. I did have a few friends who died young through disease, car wrecks, and war. But, as a daily consideration, death wasn't included. Now in my seventies, with several of my contemporaries already passed away, it's "in my face" and in my thoughts more often. And, true to what I was told by those older than I, the time has passed by so rapidly. Life is short. Wisdom is realizing that brevity of our days and, therefore, living our lives fully, here and now, and living our lives now in a way that prepares us for when it is over on this planet.

This works in a number of ways. It may be as practical as providing financially for my family when I'm gone. It includes leaving a spiritual legacy to my children and grandchildren as an exemplary follower of Jesus and as a participant in His kingdom. It may involve asking myself, in the midst of decisions or even anxieties, "Is this really going to matter in a hundred years?" It's living in the beauty and in the opportunity of each new day with Jesus. Living in wisdom means I remember I'm only here a short while, and I live accordingly. That's wisdom!

Wisdom is realizing that God's ways are the best. God's way of living will be the most beneficial and the most satisfying for us. Wisdom is appreciating this life, this brief life, He has given us and using all that He has given us (in its fullness) to bring glory to Him.

WHERE DO WE GET WISDOM?

We can parrot the answer to this question, right? It's God!

> *For the LORD gives wisdom; From His mouth*
> *come knowledge and understanding.*
>
> Pr 2:6

HOW do we acquire wisdom from God? What is the process? Maybe it would be "wise" to look at, reputedly, the wisest man in history (besides Jesus) whom I introduced in the Introduction: Solomon. Let's see how Solomon received his wisdom.

Solomon has succeeded his father, David as king of Israel. One night while Solomon was in Gibeon, the Lord appeared to him in a dream and told him to ask for anything he wanted. What would you ask for? Here's Solomon's reply:

> *So give Your servant an **understanding heart** to*
> *judge*
> *Your people to discern between good and evil.*
> *For who is able to judge this great people of Yours?*
>
> 1 Ki 3:9, emphasis added

Two verses later, the Lord answers:

> *God said to him, "Because you have asked this thing*
> *and have not asked for yourself long life, nor have*
> *asked riches for yourself, nor have you asked for the life*
> *of your enemies, but have asked for ourself discernment*
> *to understand justice, behold, I have done according*
> *to your words. Behold, I have given you a **wise and***

discerning heart, *so that there has been no one like you before you, nor shall one like you arise after you.*
1 Ki 3:11–12, emphasis added

Literally, in the Hebrew text, Solomon asks not for *"an understanding heart"* but for a *listening heart*. And God says, "Ok, I'll give you a wise and listening heart."

Of all that Solomon could ask God for, why did he ask for this? Is there anything in Solomon's upbringing, anything his father David might have told him, to prepare him to ask for such a thing? Yes, we see it when Solomon is writing to one of his sons in the book of Proverbs:

When I [Solomon] was a son to my father [David], Tender and the only son in the sight of my mother, Then he taught me and said to me, "Let your heart hold fast my words; Keep my commandments and live; Acquire wisdom! Acquire understanding! Do not forget nor turn away from the words of my mouth. "Do not forsake her, and she will guard you; Love her, and she will watch over you. "The beginning of wisdom is: Acquire wisdom; And with all your acquiring, get understanding.
Pr 4:3–7

Solomon is telling his son what his grandfather David exhorted him (Solomon) to do: Acquire wisdom! He says it: "the beginning of wisdom is: Acquire wisdom." In other words, "You gotta want it!"

To want something, you must see what the benefits are to having it. That's why I'm writing this book: to shine a spotlight on the benefits of living in and with wisdom. All through Proverbs, Solomon keeps telling his son that wisdom is more valuable than any riches (gold and silver) he could desire. Why? In a few words, the answer is: wisdom brings life.

Listen to what James says characterizes wisdom:

> *But the wisdom from above is first pure, then*
> *peaceable, gentle, reasonable, full of mercy and good*
> *fruits, unwavering, without hypocrisy.*
>
> Jas 3:17

Doesn't that sound like the kind of life you want? I'll comment on this verse a little more in the last chapter. We begin by wanting wisdom. Next, we ask for it; we seek wisdom. James is clear: "But if any of you lacks wisdom, let him ask of God, who gives to all generously and with reproach, and it will be given to him" (James 1:5). Wisdom, speaking in Proverbs 8, says, "I love those who love me; and those who diligently seek me will find me" (8:17). What a promise!

As I've pointed out before, the apostle Paul also saw the necessity of wise living and, therefore, included it in his prayers for believers.in two different churches. He says:

> *I do not cease giving thanks for you while making*
> *mention of you in my prayers; that the God of our Lord*
> *Jesus Christ, the Father of glory, may give to you a spirit*
> *of wisdom and of revelation in the knowledge of Him.*
>
> Eph 1:16–17

> *For this reason also, since the day we heard of it,*
> *we have not ceased to pray for you and to ask that you*
> *may be filled with the knowledge of His will in all*
> *spiritual wisdom and understanding ....*
>
> Col 1:9

We have been made with a spirit, a human spirit, to be a receptacle, a meeting place in our innermost being, with the Holy Spirit of God (see a full explanation of this in my book *From Deep Within: Living Out Of Our Spirit*, Burkhart Books © 2013). It is in our spirit that we can receive wisdom; it's there that we can "be filled with the knowledge of His will in all spiritual wisdom and understanding"

So, let's see the value of living in, with, and by wisdom, and let's "diligently seek" and ask for it. It's a prayer waiting to be answered!

Summary

- We are wise when we live life skillfully, using the gifts and talents given by God.
- We are wise when we follow God's laws, His ways, His guide to life.
- We are wise when we appreciate the shortness of life and live each day to the max.
- We are wise when we know:
  - What to think, say or do
  - Why I'm doing it (or refraining from doing it)
  - How to do, say, or act on it
  - When to do it
  - To whom or with whom to do it
  - Wisdom, then, is acting upon it!

In order to accomplish these things in seeing wisdom released in our lives, we will see how the seven various aspects of wisdom operate to accomplish this.

Now, let's move on in the next chapter to the first pillar of wisdom: Knowledge.

Do you appreciate and use the gifts, the talents, and abilities God has given to you? Would you ask Him for more or unique ways to use these?

Are there ways of God you have rejected and are receiving the consequences from that rejection? Are there "course corrections" that need to be made through repentance and loving obedience to Him?

Are you appreciating each day as a gift from God and living it for Him and through His power and love?

Are there things in your life about which you just need to ask for wisdom from God?

CHAPTER 3

KNOWLEDGE

Most of us know the Genesis story. God created the heavens and the earth, and all that fills them. As the crown of His creation, God creates man, male and female. He places Adam and Eve in the Garden of Eden to tend it and to have a daily, close relationship with Him, their Creator, and their Lover. He encourages them to eat from all the trees in the garden, except one, the tree of the knowledge of good and evil.

Eve, and then Adam, disobeyed, ate, and did, indeed, "know" good and evil from that point onward. The Hebrew word used here is a derivative for the verb "know," *yada*. It is a deep and rich word and calls for a deeper understanding.

Most of us in the "western culture" and as "western Christians" have been influenced by Greek thinking … more so than most of us realize. I believe it's important to see the contrast between what *knowledge* is from a Greek mindset and what it means from a Hebrew or Biblical mindset. For Greeks, knowledge was "static." That means it was a "thing," something to acquire, something to learn, grasp, and remember with your mind: a "body of knowledge." Hebrews thought knowledge was "dynamic." What we think of as a thing (knowledge) they thought of as moving and living reality. How this affects our understanding of "knowledge" is that knowledge was a *relational or living thing* (NOTE: see Heb. 4:12: "The word of God is living and active"). For most of us, to "know" the Word of God is gaining an accumulation of

37

facts, stories, and doctrinal teachings. For our spiritual ancestors, to "know" the Word of God was to experience it, to have it actively change their lives.[1]

True knowledge is gained through experience. Knowledge is relational. That is why the same word, *yada*, is used in Genesis 4:1 to describe Adam and Eve's sexual intimacy: "Now the man *knew* his wife Eve, and she conceived and gave birth ...." Knowledge, in the biblical sense, is not to just "know" data intellectually (i.e., you "know" enough to pass the exam) but it is a relational knowing, it is interaction with something alive and dynamic.

Listen to Hannah's (Samuel's mother in 1 Samuel 2:3) praise of God and speaking of His knowledge:

> *Boast no more so very proudly, Do not let arrogance come out of your mouth; For the LORD is a God of knowledge,*
> *And with Him, actions are weighed.*

With God, knowledge is not just that He "knows" stuff about (details, data) but that knowledge is related to His actions and our actions. In application, how is our knowledge of Him affecting how we live?

As it was with wisdom, "the fear of the Lord" is also the beginning of knowledge (Prov. 1:7). Since knowledge is an aspect of wisdom that stands to reason, right? To acknowledge God's rightful place in my life, to recognize His all-knowing and all-wise presence and submit myself in worship and awe and thankfulness is like opening the door to let His knowledge come into my life. There are so many things He wants to show us about Himself. Read this promise: but just as it is written:

> *"THINGS WHICH EYE HAS NOT SEEN AND*
> *EAR HAS NOT HEARD, AND which HAVE*
> *NOT ENTERED THE HEART OF MAN, ALL*
> *THAT GOD HAS PREPARED FOR THOSE*
> *WHO LOVE HIM." For to us, God revealed them*
> *through the Spirit; for the Spirit searches all things,*
> *even the depths of God.*
>
> 1 Co 2:9–10

Imagine that! Because those of us that have given our hearts to Jesus, this promise is that the Holy Spirit living within us will show us "even the depths of God." Amazing!

"Knowledge is the true representation of how things are" (Dallas Willard, from a lecture series, "Heart and Soul Conference," as quoted in *Renovated* by Dallas Williard and Jim Wilder, NavPress, © 2020, page 27). If we need to know "the true representation of how things are," what better way than to get it from God Himself? That's true knowledge.

Another way to gain knowledge is to get it from godly mentors. I say mentors rather than teachers because, being a teacher myself, teachers can convey information, head knowledge, without ever having experienced it themselves. The spiritual gift of teaching and the role of spiritual teachers (cf. Rom. 12:7; 1 Cor. 12:28; Eph. 4:11) is a supernatural gift. This means that this kind of teaching isn't just some natural ability or learned skill. Supernatural teaching can be measured by the fruit our Lord produces through its function. In other words, does the teaching produce life? Does it bring us deeper into relationship with the Father, with Jesus, and with the Holy Spirit? Does it produce the fruit of the Spirit: love, joy, peace, patience, kindness, goodness, faithfulness, gentleness, and self-control?

I remember sitting in more than one seminary class, listening to various professors or lecturers speaking about ministry. I was already in my mid-thirties, had operated a business (dental practice) as well, as participated in church life as both a congregant and as a leader. As I listened to these lectures, I was often saying to myself, "Yes, I've seen that work" or "No, that's not reality, that won't work." As I think back to the "Yes, that works" statements, those speakers were the "Been there; done that" people. They were speaking out of their own ministry experiences. The others were, perhaps, just passing on information they heard or read somewhere.

Solomon, in writing Proverbs to his son, is the "been there; done that" kind-of-guy. Repeatedly he urges his son (and, since the Scriptures are God's guide to living, our heavenly Father, through this wonderful book, urges us) to listen to him, to receive the knowledge he is writing about. In fact, Wisdom speaks to those to whom she called, and they refused, "Then they will call on Me, but I will not answer; they will seek Me diligently, but they will not find Me, because they hated knowledge and did not choose the fear of the Lord" (Prov. 1:28, 29).

This kind of knowledge comes only from the Lord and from those who have received it from the Lord. This kind of knowledge, Solomon tells his son and tells us, is "pleasant to your soul" (2:10). When we see reality, "the true representation of how things are," it often gives us a sense of peace or a sense of order, even if that knowledge isn't encouraging. If that knowledge doesn't seem encouraging, we can rest on the knowledge that God's will and counsel will win out in the end. We know that this revealed knowledge is given to us by the Lord to guide us in our responses. We can be at peace knowing we are doing His will in that or those particular circumstances.

Knowledge isn't only about WHAT you know. It's about what you put into practice (or stay away from if that knowledge is a warning!). There is a very interesting verse in Proverbs 11 (verse 9) which makes this "knowledge into practice" applicable:

> *With his mouth, the godless man destroys his neighbor, But through knowledge, the righteous will be delivered.*

What does this mean? A "godless man" (in this case, the Jewish rabbis believed Solomon was referring to a flatterer, but it could also be a gossip or false witness) will destroy someone with words. But the righteous, because that person has God's knowledge, knows how to respond (or not to respond) and be "delivered" from the godless person's schemes. To have this kind of knowledge will serve to protect us.

I can remember when I first gave my life, my heart, and my all to Jesus. The man who was discipling me gave me a hard-back copy of the New American Standard Bible, New Testament (the whole Bible in NASB wasn't finished yet). I began to read it and devour it. It was fresh. It was exciting. It spoke to my life. I started to gain knowledge, not just in my head but in my heart. I started to put that knowledge into practice. My "knowledge of the Holy" increased (see, A.W. Tozer, *Knowledge of the Holy*, HarperOne Publishing, (c)1961, for the attributes of God and our response to them). My life changed. As it did, the people around me noticed and started asking questions. Their curiosity led either to their salvation or to a re-commitment of their lives to Christ. Godly knowledge led to Godly transformation, which led to Godly practice, which led to Godly results.

We see the same theme in the New Testament. The apostle Paul prayed for the believers at Ephesus that they would receive "a spirit of wisdom and revelation in the knowledge of Him" (Eph. 1:17). It's enlightening that the Greeks had three different words for "know" or "knowledge." One word just conveys the idea of something I didn't know, and now I do. The second word speaks of the process of coming to know something. The third word means that I have learned, or know, something by experience. This is the word Paul uses in his Ephesians prayer. This same word is used later (4:13) to be equated with Christian maturity:

> ... *Until we all attain to the unity of the faith and of the **knowledge** of the Son of God, to a mature man, to the measure of the stature which belongs to the fullness of Christ.*

Maturity means we know Christ by really experiencing Him. Again, I remind you the Jesus is the foundation upon whom the pillar of knowledge rests!

To be wise is to apply knowledge. Wisdom is living life, having received from our God a "knowing" of His true reality. Wisdom is right living because I *know* what right living is. I am convinced it is the correct and most satisfying way to live, and am putting that knowledge into daily practice.

Sometimes we know the way to live, yet we don't follow through and live that way. Perhaps it's because we just want things our way. Perhaps we are deceived into thinking that our way is better or more satisfying than God's way. Perhaps we are afraid to "risk it" and live by faith and belief in what God has said. Regardless of the reason or reasons we don't follow His way, we find wisdom "the hard way." We receive the consequences of our wrong and sinful choices. It IS a hard way to learn wisdom. I've gained some of my wisdom that way; I'm sad to say. Yet our loving Father always is ready to receive us back again. Even when I have messed up, failed, and suffered for it, I can't think of a time that Father has said, "See, I told you so!" So, it's much better to learn wisdom on the "front end" than on the "back end."

The next chapter is the pillar of Understanding.

What do you "know" of God? Jot down several experiences that have helped you to know Him.

How have you put the knowledge of God and His ways into practice?

Can you put into prayer right now other ways you want to fill your spirit up with "wisdom and revelation of the knowledge of Him?"

[1]The root (*yada*) expresses knowledge gained in various ways by the senses. ... *Da'at* is a general term for knowledge, particularly that which is of a personal, experimental nature (Prov. 24:5). TWOT, Vol. I, page 366.

CHAPTER 4

UNDERSTANDING

"I understand."

Have you ever had anyone say that to you, and you KNEW, you just KNEW, they didn't understand? That's a fairly easy statement to make: "I understand." What does it mean to understand something or someone? When I teach communication, I mention four essential ingredients to good communication: a sender of the message, a means or method of communication, a receiver (are you listening?) of the message, and, finally, understanding of the message. So, understanding is crucial. If there is no understanding, clear and good communication hasn't taken place. What is understanding, and what does it look like?

We saw in Chapter 2 that Solomon's dad David told him to "Acquire wisdom! Acquire understanding!" Understanding, in the book of Proverbs, is often coupled with wisdom.

> *How blessed is the man who finds wisdom.*
> *And the man who gains understanding.*
>
> Pr 3:13

> *Say to wisdom, "You are my sister," And call*
> *understanding your intimate friend ....*
>
> Pr 7:4

*Does not wisdom call, and understanding
lift up her voice?*

Pr 8:1

*Wisdom rests in the heart of one who has understanding,
but in the hearts of fools it is made known.*

Pr 14:33

Let's find out the particular "hue" that understanding gives to the mosaic of wisdom.

The Hebrew word used in Proverbs for understanding is *binah*. It means "to realize, or to hear and apprehend information," "to think about, ponder," "to process information so as to respond in an appropriate manner."[1]

Ah! Would you have loved to have been with the disciples when, after hearing of the appearance of the resurrected Jesus to the two men on the road to Emmaus, Jesus appeared to them all? After asking for a snack (He wanted them to see that He was a real, resurrected human and not a vision), Luke 24 says:

*Now He said to them, "These are My words which
I spoke to you while I was still with you, that all
things which are written about Me in the Law
of Moses and the Prophets and the Psalms
must be fulfilled." Then He opened their minds
to understand the Scriptures,*

Lk 24:44–45

Now, when the Lord gives understanding, that's understanding! By the way, we can still ask Jesus to give us an understanding of the Scriptures.

So, identical to wisdom, understanding comes from the Lord. Also, similar to wisdom, we are to seek understanding:

Give me understanding, that I may observe Your
law and keep it with all my heart.

Ps 119:34

Make your ear attentive to wisdom, incline
your heart to understanding; for if you cry for
discernment, lift your voice for understanding ….

Pr 2:2–3

"Lift up your voice for understanding" sounds like a pretty passionate prayer to me. We will see this exhortation for all the aspects of wisdom. They are so valuable, they are so needed, that a sense of desperation must accompany our prayers for them.

I believe we can get a picture of understanding by looking at the prophet Daniel. Daniel was taken from Jerusalem to Babylon by King Nebuchadnezzar when he was a young man. Daniel, chapter 1, describes the process of how he came into the presence and confidence of the king. The king ordered his chief official to find and bring in:

… Youths in whom was no defect, who were
good-looking, showing intelligence in every branch
*of wisdom, **endowed with understanding** and*
discerning knowledge, and who had ability for serving
in the king's court; and he ordered him to teach them
the literature and language of the Chaldeans.

Dan 1:4

In other words, this chief official was to look at, perhaps interview, ask about, and otherwise find out who, of these youths, was *endowed with understanding.* How did he find this out about Daniel? What was it about Daniel that gave this servant of Nebuchadnezer the confidence to bring him into the "development program"?

This word understanding, *bin* or *binah*, also has the meaning of "to consider carefully" or "to be circumspect." Being circumspect means to be able to walk around something and see it from all sides. Somehow, someway, this official saw Daniel approaching things this way. Daniel carefully considered things, not making quick judgments. He was circumspect. He waited to reach a decision until he had seen things from all sides.

Later in the book, the young Daniel now grown old, is given visions from the Lord. He sees things. But the angel Gabriel must give him understanding of the visions (Dan. 8:16; 9:22). And, having been given understanding (the deeper meaning of what he saw) in these two instances, Daniel himself seeks understanding in the case of a third vision (Dan. 10:1 ff.).

Understanding means I go deeper than what the surface situation or person appears to be. I ask the Lord for understanding why a thing is the way it is, why a person is acting or saying the things they are. I seek to grasp a deeper meaning.

This is the point I believe Jesus was making in the parable of the four soils (Matthew 13). In the first soil, Jesus says the person hears the Word but doesn't *understand* it (13:19). Therefore, the enemy comes and steals away the Word (seed). The second and third soils are those who hear the Word but other factors negate any growth and fruit. Notice, however, that in describing the fourth soil, Jesus says the one on whom the seed was sown in good soil "hears the Word and *understands* it and bears much fruit" (13:23).

The reason some people are the "good soil" is that they hear the Word and understand it. They receive the

Word of the kingdom and understand the good news that God not only loves them and wants a relationship with them but also wants to rule and reign in their lives and empower them to live a life worthy of Him! Therefore they joyfully receive the Word.

Understanding gives meaning. Understanding correlates things together. It brings about the "Aha!" moment. Understanding makes knowledge work:

> *A scoffer seeks wisdom and finds none, but knowledge is easy to one who has understanding.*
>
> Pr 14:6

Knowledge is easily apprehended by the one who has carefully considered the situation or person they are encountering. Remember? "Knowledge is the true representation of the way things are" (Dallas Willard, quoted in Chapter 3). Understanding gets us there. God may present us with revelational knowledge. A person of understanding looks at it from all sides.

Over the course of the last three decades, the Lord has been gracious to give me revelations on many occasions. Sometimes those revelations have come through visions or dreams or hearing the Lord speak or from receiving a "word" from another spiritually gifted person. But hearing or receiving revelation may not be helpful unless there is an accurate interpretation of that revelation. Many times, when I've received something I believe is from the Lord for someone else, I have to make sure I only give them what I saw or heard UNLESS I believe the Lord has given me the interpretation of what I saw or heard. I'm usually pretty careful to tell the person the difference. In other words, I'll say, "I had this vision when I was praying for you. This is what I saw." Then, if I believe I have an interpretation (an understanding) of what I saw, I will say, "And this is what I believe it means, but pray about it yourself."

A person of understanding sees more deeply into things, including persons. That's why Proverbs 20:5 says, "A plan in the heart of a man is like deep water, but a man of understanding draws it out." A person of understanding can look deep into the heart of another, seeing how God has made and gifted them, and perhaps see some of the calling on their lives and bring encouragement to them to walk out their identity in Christ.

The person of understanding is also a receiver as well as a giver:

> *A rebuke goes deeper into one who has*
> *understanding than a hundred blows into a fool.*
>   Pr 17:10

Why does a rebuke go deeper into a person of understanding? It's because they have an understanding of themselves and an understanding of the way or ways the Lord is using that the rebuke to guide them back into the fullness He has for them. The understanding person knows that a justified rebuke is for their growth. Therefore, they don't throw up defenses, get angry (well, maybe sometimes! But eventually they realize it's for their good!), or at the other extreme, become self-condemning. They take it as a gift, a blessing, and inwardly or outwardly thank the Lord and even the one who brings the rebuke.

As I write this chapter, the streets of the United States are filled with protesters. The protesters are African-Americans, and those sympathetic, who are angered and outraged. Triggered, most recently, by the videoed deaths of African-American men at the hands of law enforcement officers, the protests are fundamentally much, much deeper. My wife and I, both being white and raised in a "white culture," have been on a journey of several years to gain understanding from our African-Americans friends. We have spent hours in conversations with them, hearing of their backgrounds and experiences. We have read books together to gain, again, understanding of one another. My wife and I have gained, in our estimation, only a small amount of understanding. But understanding goes deeper than to judge these protests from one point of view or give simple answers to the issues raised. Understanding wants to walk all the way around it, dig down below it, and to see it from above—from God's perspective.

"Tell me more. I want to understand."

Wanting to understand expresses commitment. Giving ourselves to understanding actually denotes we understand understanding!

Knowing, loving, and listening to Jesus is the foundation of the pillar of understanding.

The next chapter is the pillar: Counsel.

Have you ever passionately asked God for understanding?

Have you ever formed an opinion about something but later, with more information, had to reverse that opinion?

Is there something or someone you need to "walk all the way around" in order to understand it/them better?

[1] The Dictionary of Biblical Languages, Hebrew Old Testament, James Swanson, © 1997 Logos Research Systems, Second Edition 2001.

CHAPTER 5

COUNSEL

*It [lightning] changes direction, turning around
by His guidance, that it may do whatever He
commands it on the face of the inhabited earth.*

Job 37:12

Elihu, in addressing Job and his "friends," speaks of the greatness of God in creation. In this verse, he says that God changes the direction of lightning by His *guidance*. This is one of two main Hebrew words for "counsel." [1] Counsel is guidance. We will see, as we delve into this term, what this counsel is, where it can come from, and what its results are when received.

*Where there is no guidance the people fall, but
in abundance of counselors there is victory.*

Prov. 11:14

*Prepare plans by consultation,
and make war by wise guidance.*

Prov. 20:18

*For by wise guidance you will wage war, and in
abundance of counselors there is victory.*

Prov. 24:6

Counsel/guidance brings about victory in life, "waging war" (coming against the enemy of our souls: the world system, our own fleshly desires, and thoughts, or attacks from our enemy Satan and his demonic hordes) successfully depends on those of wisdom gathered around us to help guide us to victorious Christian living.

The second Hebrew word used for counsel gives us a bit more information and ideas about this aspect of wisdom.

> *The **counsel** of the LORD stands forever, the plans of His heart from generation to generation.*
>
> Ps. 33:11

Here, counsel is not just guidance in general, but it involves plans.[2] Plans are strategies. They are specific ways of handling situations or carrying out desires to completion. Counsel given in this way means, "Here's what I suggest: do this and do that and then do this." They involve not only the end desired result but also the means or way(s) to get there.

David had a "counselor" named Ahithophel. When David's son Absalom rebelled and came to unseat David from the throne of Israel, David fled. Left behind in Jerusalem was Ahithophel. Now David knew how wise this counselor was. He knew if Ahithophel were to give Absalom "strategies" that those would bring about David's downfall. Consequently, David prays to the Lord, "O LORD, I pray, make the counsel of Ahithophel foolishness." Ahithophel does give Absalom "wise counsel." If Absalom had listened to it, he might have overcome David. But Absalom didn't listen. Ahithophel's counsel was, indeed, considered "foolishness" to him, and David's prayer was answered. Read about this story in 2

Samuel 15:12 - 17:23. Ahithophel's counsel, had it been followed by Absalom, would have given him victory.

The way of a fool is right in his own eyes, but a wise man is he who listens to counsel.

Prov. 12:15

A wise person is one who LISTENS to counsel. To listen, we must have counselors around us—those who know the Lord, have walked with Him for a while so that their counsel comes not only from their following His ways expressed in His Word, but also have learned from experience what "works" in life and what doesn't. This kind of counsel comes from a long track record with God and seeing His faithfulness in a variety of conditions. This kind of counsel comes about when followers of Jesus tap into the "spirit of counsel," as referenced in Isaiah 11's declaration of the seven-fold Spirit of God (11:2). This kind of counsel comes from the life of Jesus expressed through these godly men and women. For, from deep within them, the One Who is called "Wonderful Counselor" (Isaiah 9:6) can speak.

Sometimes that counsel contains reproof. Sometimes we must have a "course correction" in our lives, and that correction or reproof comes through the words of a faithful friend and counselor. My wife has filled this role more than once in my life! I often tell people, "I often hear the voice of the Holy Spirit, and many times He sounds just like my wife!" One of the best bits of counsel Suzanne has given me over the years is to remind me that most people don't "catch" something the first time I share it. I've got to repeat the vision, outlook, or strategy many, many times to communicate it well. I naturally don't do that. I figure if I've said it, it's communicated. Listening to my wife's counsel has aided me in my leadership.

I've been blessed to have a number of other "counselors" over the years. They have been men and women who know the Lord, have gotten to know me (and I have gotten to know them), and have traveled a similar road in life that I have traveled and am traveling. By 2013 I had been the lead pastor for over 28 years. The immediate past 14 years, we (the church fellowship) had been located in an area of Dallas, just east of downtown, called Deep Ellum. During those years, we had our meetings in several rented locations. In the summer of 2013, the owner of the space we were leasing sold it to a development group. When I heard the news, I was anticipating a call from the new owners and, sure enough, received it. In a meeting shortly thereafter, I was told we would have to move out of our space since they were renovating and changing the area. As I had done so many times before, I began to pray and drive the streets of Deep Ellum, looking for a new space. After I had made several trips over the course of several days and found nothing, I realized something else.

The Lord had always given me direction in times like these, especially in re-location. This time, not only did I not have any direction about rental space, I realized I didn't have any direction for the future of the fellowship. This had never happened in over 28 years. One of my mentors, years previously, had advised me that when you don't see God doing something, take a step backward and see what He IS doing. When I did that, I saw that the Lord had been connecting me with younger pastors and leaders to step into the role of advisor, counselor, mentor, or spiritual father with them.

About that time, I went to a retreat with my spiritual father, Jack Taylor, and several other men whom I had known for several years. Papa Jack is one of the wisest men I know. When I told him where I was—without a vision for the church but repeatedly being connected to these young leaders—I asked Jack if he thought the Lord was leading me to turn the church over to someone else and "go after" these leaders full time. He said, "John, you're not going to be happy doing anything else!"

Jack's counsel was the deciding factor in the transition I made at that time. I returned home, gathered the church leadership team together, and told them what was going on. They all said they knew this was going to happen someday. One of the leader couples took over as pastors of the church, and I stepped out into the next phase of my ministry life.

Wise and godly counsel is a necessary ingredient that our Lord uses to give us direction. Remember what Proverbs 12:15 says about the "fool"? He is so sure that his way is THE way he won't listen to counsel. A person who won't listen to or seek counsel is going to live a hit-and-miss life, at best, and, at worst, will find themselves in lots of trouble!

Experiencing Jesus, more and more, is the foundation of the pillar of counsel.

The next chapter is the pillar: Prudence.

Do you have one or more people you can count on for counsel? If not, will you pray and ask God to put those people in your life or direct you to them?

Can you think of a time when someone offered you, counsel, you took it, and it proved beneficial to you?

Can you think of a time when someone tried to offer counsel, you didn't listen, and paid for it?

¹[הַלְבֹחֵת] n.f. direction, counsel (prob. orig. of rope-pulling, i.e. steering, directing a ship, Brown, F., Driver, S. R., & Briggs, C. A. (1977). *Enhanced Brown-Driver-Briggs Hebrew and English Lexicon* (p. 287). Oxford Edition.

²6783 I. יָעַץ ('ē·sā(h)): **advice**, counsel, i.e., the act. of telling someone what they should do based on a plan or scheme (2Sa 15:34), Swanson, J. (1997). *Dictionary of Biblical Languages with Semantic Domains: Hebrew (Old Testament)* (electronic ed.). Oak Harbor: Logos Research Systems, Inc.

CHAPTER 6

PRUDENCE

The proverbs of Solomon ...
to give prudence to the naïve ....

Prov. 1:1, 4)

I, Wisdom, dwell with prudence ....

Prov. 8:12

Another aspect of wisdom is prudence. The Hebrew word for prudence is *ormah,* which comes from a word which means "to see or understand the highest or most important strength." Prudence is putting understanding into action by finding the strongest and most effective response in a unique kind of situation.

It's very interesting to see prudence in action in two Scripture passages outside of the book of Proverbs. I believe looking at these two instances will help us understand and apply prudence in our lives.

The first story is found in Joshua, chapter 9. Leading up to this story, Joshua has led the children of Israel into the land of promise, Canaan. They have defeated their enemies in Jericho, Ai (after one setback), and Bethel. They are carrying out the Lord's command to defeat all the inhabitants of the land. When the kings of the people groups (Hittite, Amorite, Canaanite, Perizzite,

Hivite, and Jebusite) heard of Israel's victories, they joined themselves together to fight against the Lord's people.

However, when the residents of Gibeon heard the same reports, they took a different tactic. They disguised themselves as travelers from a distant land, carrying worn-out sacks, patched clothing and sandals, and moldy bread as if they had been on a long journey getting to where Joshua and Israel were camped. They came and deceived Joshua into believing they weren't from Canaan and requested a peace treaty. Joshua agreed (never asking the Lord about it, cf. 9:14!) and made a peace treaty with them. Three days later, Israel found out who they really were but stood by their promise and did not kill them but made them servants.

Why do I bring up this story in reference to prudence? In Joshua 9:4, it says that these Gibeonites "acted craftily." "Craftily" here is the Hebrew word for prudence. The Gibeonites realized that they were going to be defeated by Israel unless some kind of drastic, "strong" action prevented that from happening. They were crafty, or prudent, a form of wisdom which acts in light of a dire situation.

The second story shows us something similar. In Luke 16, Jesus tells the parable of what is known as "the unrighteous steward" (16:1-9). In this story, there is a rich man who had a "manager" or "steward" who took care of his master's affairs, including his financial dealings and agreements with others. Apparently, the rich owner had not checked on the accounting books in a long time (or ever). But he receives word that his manager has mishandled his affairs. An accounting is requested. Later in the story, Jesus calls the steward or manager "unrighteous" (verse 8), so He is not condoning what the manager did. The manager, in a panic, decides that he must do something drastic in order to preserve himself after his lord fires him (he is expecting the worst to happen!). So, the manager calls the debtors of the lord and, one by one, reduces their debt on the books, thus putting himself in the good graces of the debtors. When his master comes back and finds out what the manager did, he (according to Jesus telling this story), "praised the unrighteous manager because he acted *shrewdly* (a word for *prudently*)."

Jesus uses this parable to teach His disciples to use worldly possessions to benefit others "so that when it (worldly wealth or money) fails, they will receive you into the eternal dwellings." As Jesus goes on to explain in the following verses, our use of money (which He terms "a very little thing" in verse 10) is a revealing factor of our heart to follow the Lord and His ways.

Again, from the parable of the unrighteous manager, we see that prudence is acting wisely in a catastrophic or crucial situation. This manager found himself in an awful predicament. His "strong" action is termed shrewd or prudent. Prudence is applied understanding (often in creative ways) to provide a solution or response.

There are situations that arise in our lives that are life-threatening or financially-threatening or perhaps even relationally-threatening. Something must be done! As we seek the Lord, He can give us His ideas (many times very creative ideas we would never have thought of) to provide an answer or a way out of the situation. This is righteous prudence. It takes into account a proper understanding of what is going on. The unrighteous steward correctly evaluated his situation. He knew if he were found out, he would be out on the street. But then he said, "I know what I shall do ..." (16:4). He had a prudent idea. We may not agree with his actions, but we can agree, with his lord, that he acted shrewdly or prudently.

Another New Testament "story" can give us insight on prudence. In Matthew 24 and 25, Jesus is answering the disciples' question about when He will return and set up His kingdom. After telling them of a series of events leading up to His return, He tells them three parables about being ready though He may delay in coming. The middle parable is about ten virgins who await the coming of the bridegroom. Jesus calls five of these girls "foolish." The other five He calls "prudent." You probably know the story: there is a delay in His return. The foolish took no extra oil with them for their lamps. The prudent ones took extra. The lamps of the foolish burned out. But the prudent had oil and light enough to welcome the bridegroom. Why did Jesus call these five "prudent"? These were those who were prepared for the unseen emergency (the delayed arrival of the bridegroom). This again shows us that prudence is the aspect of wisdom which knows how to respond to a situation with "strength."

TWO STORIES FROM MY WIFE ABOUT PRUDENCE

A few years ago, my wife was a Community Director for a ministry in a low-income, high-crime apartment complex. The ministry, among other things, had an after-school tutoring and discipleship time for children. Suzanne found out one day that one of the teenage girls had been posting some awful things on social media about another girl who lived in the same apartments and had some handicaps. Suzanne knew if she confronted the first girl about her posts that she would meet with resistance. So, taking encouragement from the story of the prophet Nathan when he confronted King David about his sin with Bathsheba (2 Samuel 11), she sat the teen down one afternoon.

Suzanne: "I want to tell you a story. One day a boy arrived here with a puppy he had found. The puppy had an injured leg. As we talked, the boy began to kick and kick the poor puppy."

Teen: "Oh! That's awful!"

Suzanne: "The boy kept kicking the poor little puppy!"

Teen (very upset): "Who is that boy?"

Suzanne: "It's you!"

Suzanne then told her how she had, essentially, been kicking an injured puppy by what she had said on social media about the other girl. The teenager was responsive to Suzanne's rebuke by way of the story rather than my wife just jumping in and confronting her directly, which would have caused her defenses to go up.

A similar thing happened during a field trip to Washington, D.C. Suzanne and some other staff members of the ministry took a group of teens to our nation's capital on a "Black Heritage Tour." While in D.C., the group had to wait in line to enter a restaurant. While they waited, one of the boys kept getting out of line. When addressed by another staff member, a vocal tug-of-war started: "Get back in line!" "No!" "Get back in line!" "No!" This went on for several minutes.

Finally, Suzanne took the young man aside and sat down with him. She told him a story, a real story which happened to her. One day at the Community Center, a young girl came in with a snotty attitude. Suzanne got in her face to correct her. That night as Suzanne was getting into bed, the Lord gave her a vision. In the vision, she was looking at a collage. From a distance, the collage looked like a picture of Jesus. As Suzanne got closer, though, she could see the picture was composed of hundreds of smaller pictures of people. In the middle was a picture of the young girl Suzanne had sternly rebuked. As she caught sight of the girl's picture, the Lord said, "When you did it to _____, you did it to Me." The next day Suzanne rushed over to the young girl's apartment, told her about the vision, and asked her forgiveness for the way she corrected her. The young girl threw her arms around Suzanne and hugged her. They are still friends today after several years.

When Suzanne told this young man in D.C. about the story, she asked him if he had been disrespectful to the staff member the way Suzanne had treated the young girl. He agreed that he had been. Suzanne then asked him to do with the staff member what she had done with the young girl.

In both of these stories, my wife fleshed out what prudence looks like. If she had tried to confront either of these God-loved young people directly, she would have, no doubt, been met with resistance. Suzanne used this aspect of wisdom to know how to get around a relational roadblock and get to the person with love when their defenses were down. That's a prudent wife!

Jesus calls the person who builds their house on the rock "wise" (the word for prudent) in Matthew 7:25. This is the person who hears Jesus' words and ACTS upon them.[1]

Again, it's our relationship with and response to Jesus, which is the foundation of the pillar of prudence.

The next chapter is the pillar: Discernment.

If you have to confront someone or address an issue, do you just "barge right in" or do you ask the Lord for His approach?

Have you ever had a "dire situation" in which the Lord gave you a unique or creative way to solve it?

Ask Him to remind you, the next time you have a tough decision to make, about a prudent way to handle it!

[1]"The prudent one does not vaunt his knowledge (Prov. 12:230, ignores an insult (Prov. 12:16), acts with knowledge (Prov. 14:8), looks where he is going (Prov. 14:15), sees danger and acts appropriately (Prov. 22:30; 27:12) and is crowned with knowledge (Prov. 14:18)." TWOT, Vol. II, pp 697-698.

CHAPTER 7

DISCERNMENT

Discernment is, properly, an aspect of understanding. In many English translations of the Bible, these words are interchangeable (they come from the same Hebrew word). Yet, as we look at many of the contexts of passages where "discern" or "discernment" are used, we see it as a part of understanding that is greatly needed. Let's return to Solomon's prayer request in 1 Kings 3:9:

> *So give Your servant an understanding heart to judge Your people to **discern between good and evil**. For who is able to judge this great people of Yours?"*

Understanding, walking all around a situation or person, and getting a 360-degree view of it or them, can give us a fuller picture. One of the Hebrew derivatives of this word "discernment" is a preposition, which means "between." So, discernment then is a sifting process, as Solomon pointed out, between good and evil, true and false, and what is profitable and what isn't of the whole that we see. Discernment is knowing the source of what we are gaining from understanding.

> *For if you cry for **discernment**, Lift your voice for understanding; If you seek her as silver And search for her as for hidden treasures;*

*Then you will **discern** the fear of the LORD*
And discover the knowledge of God.

Prov. 2:3–5

Solomon is instructing his son to be earnest in seeking discernment and understanding. Seeking the things of God is the prelude to finding the things of God. Seeking discernment brings about the ability to ***discern*** the fear of the LORD. Sometimes it takes the Spirit of the Lord to impart discernment to us so that we sift out what is true about God and what we've been told or what we have, distortedly, believed. Many grow up with the idea that God is strictly a frowning judge who is waiting, just waiting, for us to step out of line so He can punish us. Although, as I've said before, the fear of the Lord does have an element of sober recognition of the greatness and power and holiness of God, He is, at the same time, a merciful, gracious, and loving heavenly Father. Discernment is used to divide out what is truth and what is error in our beliefs about God.

It not only applies to our beliefs about God; discernment is also needed in our beliefs about ourselves. David laments:

Who can discern his errors? Acquit me of hidden faults.

Ps 19:12

Without God's help, the loving confrontation of the Holy Spirit in our lives, we would overlook, brush off, or be unconscious of those things which grieve Him. David is realizing his own inability to look into his life and activity and find those faults which keep him distant from God. He is asking God to forgive even those "faults" in himself that he can't discern or sort out.

On the other hand, Solomon warns:

Leave the presence of a fool,
or you will not discern words of knowledge.

Prov. 14:7

A fool, in the book of Proverbs, is a person who knows better. They, in contrast to the naive or simple one, have been given the truth, the best way to live, God's way. Yet they decide, even knowing God's will and ways, to abandon all that and walk their own way. Therefore, this Proverbs 14 warning explains why if we stay in the presence of such a person, we won't be able to discern or sift out any truth from what they are saying. The longer we stay around them, the foggier things get. It gets harder and harder to discern truth and error. In other words, it pays to "discern" the kind of people you hang out with!

Listen to this wonderful prayer that the apostle Paul prays for the church in Philippi:

And this I pray, that your love may abound
still more and more in real knowledge and all
***discernment**, so that you may approve the things*
that are excellent, in order to be sincere and
blameless until the day of Christ; having been filled
with the fruit of righteousness which comes through
Jesus Christ, to the glory and praise of God.

Phil. 1:9–11

See the sifting effect of discernment? "…all discernment, so that you may approve the things that are excellent." Not all things are excellent that we come into contact with or think each day. It takes Godly discernment to find those excellent things. You see this in the book of Hebrews as well:

*But solid food is for the mature, who because of practice
have their senses trained to discern good and evil.*

Heb 5:14

I believe this quality of wisdom is seen also in one of the spiritual gifts given to believers. In the list of gifts in 1 Corinthians 12:10, we see one of those gifts as "distinguishing of spirits." Robert Young, in his Young's Literal Translation of the Bible (1862), uses the word "discernment" concerning this gift: "discernment of spirits." As we live among people, both people of the world and people in the church (including ourselves), there are three sources of "spirits" that may affect us. First, there is our own spirit. We can be motivated in our speech, decisions, and actions by what's in our own spirit. The second source of "spirits" is we can be affected by demonic spirits. Because we tolerate or are being attacked by our enemy's forces, again, our lives and interaction can be distorted. The third source of "spirits" is the Holy Spirit. The "distinguishing of spirits" gift is finding the source of speech or action as to whether it is coming from the human spirit, a demonic spirit (or spirits), or the Holy Spirit.

When walking about, a person with this gift can often tell from which "spirit" or source a person is operating. Many years ago, there was a man in our church fellowship. He seemed to be a great guy - enthusiastic about the Lord, worship, prayer, and fellowship with other believers. However, both my wife and another good friend would have their "spiritual radar" go into alarm mode whenever they were around this man. There was, at the time, no visible reason to suspect him of any wrongdoing. Rather than suspect him or confront him about this vague "something" as the lead pastor of the church, I just waited, prayed, and watched. However, not too many weeks down the line, it was discovered this man was living in an immoral sexual relationship with a woman from our fellowship. I see this as the exercise of this gift. My wife's and this other person's "discernment" or "distinguishing" was at the spiritual level.

I believe it is always a good practice to have someone else check our "discernment" from time to time. This is where the aspect of counsel comes into play. It takes maturity to exercise discernment. Too often, people say they are "discerning" when they are really judging or exercising a critical spirit. Did you notice that in Hebrews 5:14, it says, "who because of practice have their senses trained to discern good and evil." It takes practice. Practice discernment!

As we grow more deeply in love with Jesus, He gives us discernment. He is the foundation of the pillar of discernment!

The next chapter is the pillar: Discretion.

Have you ever taken the time while listening to a podcast or watching a video, or reading a book, to ask for discernment about what is being said or written?

Do you have your own story in which the exercise of discernment "paid off" for you or for another's spiritual benefit?

Would you ask the Lord to give you "all spiritual understanding and discernment so that you may approve the things that are excellent?"

CHAPTER 8

DISCRETION

The Hebrew word for "discretion" means "to purpose, to plan, or to scheme."[1] What this aspect of wisdom enables us to do is to plot a course of action for our lives wisely.

> *Discretion will guard you, understanding will watch over you, to deliver you from the way of evil, from the man who speaks perverse things ....*
>
> Prov. 2:11–12

As you can read from these verses, discretion is closely linked with understanding as well. *Understanding* gives us a fuller picture of the situation. *Discernment* enables us to sort out the "wheat from the chaff," the good from the bad. *Discretion* then, on the basis of this information, plots the steps we take as a result of this wisdom. Discretion, according to these verses, finds a "deliverance," a way out of harm's way, and "the man who speaks perverse things." Perverse means "that which is turned away from what is right or good," "improper," or "incorrect."

Job, in responding to the Lord (Who finally answers him in the last chapters of the book), says,

> *Then Job answered the LORD and said,*
> *"I know that You can do all things,*
> *And that no **purpose** of Yours can be thwarted.*
>
> Job 42:1–2

The Hebrew word here translated "purpose" is the word for discretion. God's plans, His purposes, what He had plotted and laid out to be accomplished—His discretion—cannot be stopped. Discretion gives us the "how" of a solution. Knowing what I know, knowing what is good, and the best outcome for my life, how do I now accomplish this? Conversely, what steps do I take to stay away from what will hinder me in accomplishing the purpose God has for me?

We see the quality of discretion worked out in Solomon's life, particularly in his plans to build the temple. First, in 1 Chronicles 22:12, we read that David expressed his desire that his son Solomon have discretion:

> *Only the LORD give you discretion and understanding, and give you charge over Israel, so that you may keep the law of the LORD your God.*

And God did! Years later, when Solomon is ready to build the temple, he sends his *plan* to Huram, the king of Tyre. He gives Huram very specific instructions about how the temple is to be built. When Huram received Solomon's message, he responds:

> *Then Huram continued, "Blessed be the LORD, the God of Israel, who has made heaven and earth, who has given King David a wise son, endowed with **discretion** and understanding, who will build a house for the LORD and a royal palace for himself.*
> 2 Ch 2:12

Huram recognizes not only Solomon's wisdom, not only Solomon's understanding, but he recognizes

Solomon's discretion by the specific plans, the "how tos," of the construction of the temple.

> *My son, give attention to my wisdom, incline your*
> *ear to my understanding; that you may observe*
> *discretion, and your lips may reserve knowledge.*
>   Pr 5:1–2

Do you see the interaction of these facets of wisdom in these verses—Wisdom, understanding, discretion, and knowledge? They all work together to make one live as the Lord planned for him or her to live.

We see this "living according to purpose" in Jesus' life.

Jesus has just had an exhausting but spiritually "successful" day in Capernaum. The crowds gathered as they brought the sick and demonized to Him, and He healed them all. But early the next morning, when the disciples arose to start "Day 2" of the Capernaum Revival, they couldn't find their Master. After a search, they found Him out, in a lonely place, praying. I assume they were getting Him to return to the village to keep doing what He had done the day before. However, Jesus says to them,

> *But He said to them, "I must preach the kingdom of God*
> *to the other cities also, for I was sent for this purpose." So*
> *He kept on preaching in the synagogues of Judea.*
>   Lk 4:43–44

Jesus, because He knew of God's purpose for Him (either the overall purpose of His first Advent or a "refresher" on purpose from the Father during His time of prayer), knew what to choose to do and what to stop doing or refrain from doing. In order to carry out God's

BIG plan for the Savior's ministry, Jesus carries out a more immediate plan to redirect His attention to Judea. Jesus exercised discretion about what to do and what not to do.

We even see Shakespeare, in one of his plays (Henry IV) saying: "Discretion is the better part of valor." What this means is that it is better to be careful than to do something that is dangerous and unnecessary to "prove our valor (or bravery)."

When I was a young kid growing up, I did a lot of stupid things to "prove my valor." In other words, I used no discretion! My guardian angel had to work overtime on several occasions to protect me!

Quite a long time ago (25-30 years ago), I had a friend who owned a lawn sprinkler business. It was during a time of recession when that industry was hard-hit. A lot of similar businesses were suffering financially. My friend decided to go away, be alone with God for several days, and ask the Lord for wisdom to know how to navigate the times. While away, the Lord answered. The type of wisdom He showed my friend was five specific things to do in his business. My friend came home, put the steps into practice, and his business prospered in a poor economy. I see this as an example of discretion because the Lord's wisdom here was to give my friend the "how to's" to successfully see his business "make it" in hard times.

What my friend did was to 1) take time out to seek the Lord; 2) pray; but 3) pray, asking for specific details that he could implement in his business, and 4) he carried out the Lord's "plan."

Our Lord can give detailed instructions. We see a multitude of examples in the Scriptures: His plans for the building of the tabernacle and later the temple, His plans about how Israel was to cross the Jordan river, His specific battle plans for David, and how Jesus wanted the gospel to go to the nations: first Jerusalem, then Judea, then Samaria, then to the ends of the earth (Matt. 28:18-20).

"Lord, what do I do now?" is as good a prayer for discretion that I know of! I've prayed that prayer on many, many occasions. God has been faithful to answer or to direct me to the answer so many times.

This ability to have discretion comes from our conversations with Jesus. He is the foundation of the pillar of discretion.

We will now look at the final pillar of Wisdom's house Instruction.

Do you have a decision to be made? Have you obtained understanding of the situation? Have you used discernment to see which is the best outcome desired by God? Have you then asked for discretion as to the next steps to take?

Do you have a friend or family member who is in need of specific details or plans from the Lord? Can you share what you've learned about this process with them and pray with them for these aspects of wisdom be given to them?

---

[1]2372 זָמַם (zā·mam): plan, plot, intend, i.e., to think with the purpose of planning or deciding a course of action Swanson, J. (1997). *Dictionary of Biblical Languages with Semantic Domains : Hebrew (Old Testament)* (electronic ed.). Oak Harbor: Logos Research Systems, Inc.

Chapter 9

INSTRUCTION

In the Introduction, I mention that at least some (perhaps most!) of the wisdom I have has been received by the way that hurts more. It's wisdom gained from making mistakes, taking the wrong road, or just plain failing. But it was wisdom GAINED in these ways, not lost, because I was "instructed" by these mistakes, misadventures, and failures. This Hebrew word "instruction" in Proverbs is a very rich word. It means "discipline," "chastening," or "correction." But it is correction that results in the person being educated. Without instruction, we would be in a very sad state, indeed, like a rebellious child who doesn't receive or hasn't received the correction that is needed in his or her life. The only other way we wouldn't need instruction is that we"d have to be perfect!

> The proverbs of Solomon, the son of David, king of
> Israel: To know wisdom and instruction,
> To discern the sayings of understanding,
> To receive instruction in wise behavior,
> Righteousness, justice, and equity ...
>
> Prov. 1:1–3

Solomon knew his son was going to mess up! God, our Father, knows we're going to mess up too! That's why we need instruction: if we will receive it! And that's why Solomon pleads with his son to receive his instruction

(Prov. 1:8; 4:1). It's even a plea from the mouth of Wisdom herself, "Heed instruction and be wise, and do not neglect it. (Prov. 8:33). In fact, it's the "fool" who despises instruction and won't receive it (1:7; 5:2). Solomon has written this word "instruction" thirteen times in Proverbs. He thought it was important! Closely connected with this instruction is learning from the Old Testament Law (Torah). In fact, in Proverbs 4;1, 2 has both words for "instruction:"

> *Hear, O sons, the instruction* (correction) *of a father, And give attention that you may gain understanding, For I give you sound teaching; Do not abandon my instruction* (Torah, Law).

In the Law, God presented Israel with a way of living that would be most beneficial for them and pleasing to Him. The various laws within the Law were not only to keep Israel safe and prosperous but also to keep them protected from the ravages of sin (spiritually), from ravages of their enemies (physically), and from idolatry. At the root of the Law was God's love, lovingly "instructing" His people, correcting them when and where necessary, to woo them into a close fellowship with Him to receive the benefits of that relationship. He knew they would mess up too. He knew, and several Old Testament saints knew that the Law could only be followed by His people loving Him back and letting that love (and dependence on His grace) motivate them to obey Him.

> *For the lips of a priest should preserve knowledge, and men should seek instruction* (Torah = law) *from his mouth; for he is the messenger of the LORD of hosts.*
>
> Mal 2:7

So, for the Old Testament saint, instruction (correction, discipline) was found in the Law (Torah). The most profound instruction from the Law was that it was to lead us (tutor us) to Christ (Galatians 3:23, 24). The same is true for us, New Testament believers. In God's word, both Old Testament and New, He has laid out for us "the handbook to life." He created us and, as the Creator, He knows the best way, the most satisfying and enjoyable and profitable way, for us to live. Jesus said, "If you love Me, you will keep my commandments." Note: He did not say, "If you keep My commandments, you will love me." Love is the motivator. And when we don't keep His commandments (in other words, when we sin), and when He comes to correct us, will we receive that correction?

> *... And you have forgotten the exhortation which is addressed to you as sons, "MY SON, DO NOT REGARD LIGHTLY THE DISCIPLINE OF THE LORD, NOR FAINT WHEN YOU ARE REPROVED BY HIM; FOR THOSE WHOM THE LORD LOVES HE DISCIPLINES; AND HE SCOURGES EVERY SON WHOM HE RECEIVES." It is for discipline that you endure; God deals with you as with sons; for what son is there whom his father does not discipline?*
>
> Heb 12:5–7

Occasionally, when someone would tell me that they were having a hard time sensing the love of God, I would quote this verse to them and ask, "Have you 'regarded lightly' the discipline of the Lord? Have you resisted that discipline? Those whom He loves, every son (or daughter), He disciplines." Perhaps this person didn't sense God's love because they were resistant to His "disciplinary love." This is certainly not the only reason people cannot sense God's love, but it's one of the reasons.

God loves us! He wants us to stay on the path to life:

> *He is on the path of life who heeds instruction,*
> *but he who ignores reproof goes astray.*
>
> Prov. 10:17–18

The beauty of God's love is that if we do go astray, His Spirit comes to us with reminders, with reproofs, with warnings, and offers to guide us back onto "the path of life." Israel ignored it or shunned it: "They have turned their back to Me and not their face; though I taught them, teaching again and again, they would not listen and receive instruction" (Jer. 32:33). We, however, can gratefully accept it.

Through hearing God, through encouragement from several counselors, through observing how the Lord was using me to produce spiritual fruit in others, and by realizing what was giving me life and satisfaction, in 1981, I decided to enroll in seminary. At the time, I was still a full-time dentist. My plan was to take a few classes each semester and continue to be at my dental office full time as long as it took to get my Master of Theology degree.

One night, shortly after my first seminary semester started, I couldn't sleep. I arose and went downstairs to the dining table with my Bible. I sought the Lord in a manner that I had been warned against. I plopped open the Bible, and without looking, just put my finger down on the page. Here are the verses I saw as I looked down. I read:

> *Therefore be careful how you walk, not as unwise*
> *men but as wise, making the most of your time*

because the days are evil. So then do not be foolish,
but understand what the will of the Lord is.

Eph 5:15–17

At that moment, reading those verses, I was "instructed" by our Lord. He gave me a "course correction." To make "the most of my time," I was to reverse my plan. I was to go to seminary full time in order to finish my course work more quickly and become a part-time dentist.

Now, don't get me wrong here! I'm not advocating using this method on a regular basis to determine the will of the Lord. After this incident, I ran my conclusion by several mature people for their input and wise counsel. But my heavenly Father was kind to show me in this manner that I wasn't progressing the way He desired for me.

Instruction gives course correction, and so many times, as in this story, the Lord uses His Word, the Scriptures, to bring that correction.

How often do we see Jesus "correcting" the disciples and others through His instruction? He still does! Jesus is the foundation of the pillar of instruction.

Having considered all the seven pillars of Wisdom's House? Let's now receive her invitation to enter the next chapter.

Are you "open" to being corrected or disciplined by the Lord's instruction?

When was the last time you experienced this kind of wisdom-gaining from the Lord?

Think of three Scriptures that have corrected or disciplined you in the past. Are there any words from the Lord doing that right now?

CHAPTER 10

ACCEPTING THE INVITATION

¹Wisdom has built her house,
she has hewn out her seven pillars;
²She has prepared her food,
she has mixed her wine;
she has also set her table;
³She has sent out her maidens,
she calls from the tops of the heights of the city:
⁴"Whoever is naive, let him turn in here!"
To him who lacks understanding she says,
⁵"Come, eat of my food and drink of the wine
I have mixed.
⁶"Forsake your folly and live, and proceed
in the way of understanding."

Prov. 9:1–6

I trust you have come to have a deeper appreciation for these seven aspects of wisdom:

Knowledge: *a relational, experiential knowing*
Understanding: *getting a 360-degree perspective*
Counsel: *guidance to bring about victory*
Prudence: *finding a strong solution in dire circumstances*
Discernment: *sorting out between good and bad*
Discretion: *choosing the right strategy*
Instruction: *correcting our path, discipline*

Wisdom's house is built. The foundation is Jesus Christ. Upon these seven "pillars," the roof or covering of wisdom rests. It takes the exercise of all seven to receive the full covering and enjoyment of Wisdom. God's wisdom is displayed in and through our lives when one, some, or all of these are functioning.

Wisdom is offering an invitation to us. Do you see it in verses 5 and 6? I believe she offers it daily. "Come into my house. Let me feed you and give you drink. Let me sustain you. I want to give you the fullness of life that the Father has designed for you. Yes, I want you to live strong; I want you to live fully."

Will we accept that invitation? To accept it, you will have to admit you are "naive" (verse 4). That is, you don't know some things. You'll have to admit that you lack understanding. So, will you join me in going, daily, to the house of Wisdom? Will you listen to the voice of the Holy Spirit as He offers to give you whatever aspect or aspects of wisdom that you need at the moment?

I repeat the verse from James:

> *But if any of you lacks wisdom, let him ask of God,*
> *who gives to all generously and without reproach,*
> *and it will be given to him.*
>
> Jas 1:5

"Let him ask of God ... and it will be given to him." So, ask! Go to our God repeatedly, often, to seek wisdom. "It will be given to him"—that's a promise! Our Lord promises us that if we will ask Him for wisdom, He will give it. Therefore, once you've asked, be alert to the ways He will answer that prayer for wisdom: through the Scriptures, through wise people (hang out with them!), and through hearing His voice and getting direction.

James, a little later on in his letter, makes two stunning comments about wisdom. The first:

> *Who among you is wise and understanding?*
> *Let him show by his good behavior his deeds*
> *in the gentleness of wisdom.*
>
> Jas 3:13

What is James telling us? He is saying that wisdom isn't just a bunch of abstract information to be stored in our brains. He is saying that wisdom, true wisdom, is lived out. That's one of the definitions of wisdom, right? It's skillful living. "In the gentleness of wisdom"—gentleness is the quality of humility, of courtesy. When we ACT on the wisdom we've been given, we don't clang a bell or shout a boast or do anything that might draw attention to ourselves. Any wisdom we can share with others is for their benefit and for God's glory.

The second stunning comment is the contrast between wisdom "not from above" and wisdom that "is from above:"

> *This wisdom is not that which comes down*
> *from above but is earthly, natural, demonic.*
> *For where jealousy and selfish ambition exist,*
> *there is disorder and every evil thing. But the*
> *wisdom from above is first pure, then peaceable,*
> *gentle, reasonable, full of mercy and good fruits,*
> *unwavering, without hypocrisy.*
>
> Jas 3:15–17

Note: There is a "wisdom not from above," and it looks like this:

- Earthly: *concerned with the here and now and self*
- Natural: *limited, doesn't take into account or believe in supernatural*
- Demonic: *motivated by the enemy to try to thwart God's will*
- *The results are jealousy, selfish ambition, disorder, every evil thing.*

Note: The contrast with "wisdom from above" which looks like:

- Pure: *coming from God, no distortions or lies*
- Peaceable: *produces peace and confidence and lives out of that*
- Gentle: *submissive to God's will, treating others as He would*
- Reasonable: *willing to be "reasoned with" or instructed and corrected*
- Full of mercy: *treating others as God would, including ourselves*
- Unwavering: *confidence in God's way and sticking to it*
- Without hypocrisy: *acting in truth without "faking it"*
- *The result is the "seed" sown in peace by peacemakers produces the fruit of righteousness.*

That's what God's wisdom looks like lived out! It produces the "fruit," the result, of right living, living according to God's plan and pleasure. This wisdom is not worked while being stressed or worried, or fearful. It is simply trusting that God and His wisdom is the best way to live.

So, let's begin to live that way! I end by praying the prayer I quoted earlier from the apostle Paul to the church at Ephesus. I pray this for you:

I ... do not cease giving thanks for you, while
making mention of you in my prayers; that the God
of our Lord Jesus Christ, the Father of glory, may
give to you a spirit of wisdom and of revelation in
the knowledge of Him.

Eph 1:16–17

May your spirit be filled with wisdom! Amen!

AN AFTERWORD

First, I want to make a major disclaimer. Although I studied Hebrew in seminary and have done a multitude of word and phrase studies in the language, even though I have two wonderful Jewish believers who've led me to fall in love with the depth of the meanings of Hebrew words and even the Hebrew letters as tutors, I am NOT a Hebrew scholar. In presenting my studies and thoughts on these different aspects of wisdom, I'm just offering the fruits of my labors and thoughts, my prayers, and stories of the applications as I've seen them and offering them to you, the reader, as helpful suggestions. A person most certainly does not have to know the Biblical languages to fall in love with Jesus, to have a deep, intimate relationship with Him, or to know, study, meditate upon, pray and apply His Word. But I've experienced Him in more depth, many times when helped by those who know Greek (the manuscript of the New Testament) and Hebrew (the manuscript of the Old Testament) and utilize them to teach supernaturally. Understanding some of the Greek and Hebrew has transformed my mind and my heart. This is not a scholarly work but written for my family, friends, and those who just want to walk more wisely through this God-given life. May it be so!

Second, I believe I received direction from the Lord to end the book with words from Him. I have been journaling for years (at least 35 years! I have boxes and boxes of journals!). In my journals, I record my thoughts, my experiences, my reactions to my experiences, my questions for the Lord, and what, I believe, He says to me. The day before yesterday, I finished the first edit of my manuscript for this book. As I finished, I asked the question, "Is this enough?" Recently, I received a phone call from one of my spiritual sons who hears from the Lord often. He said to me, "The Lord told me to call you and tell you, 'No, it's not enough.'" This young man said that those words are not how he talks, nor did he think he had ever heard something like that to tell anyone. This man did not know I had asked my question the day before. When I told him about my question, I said, "Well, I guess I have the answer. I'm trying to think if the Lord means that what I have written is enough, but not enough until He moves upon it and uses it in the lives of people. OR that what I have written really isn't enough content, and He wants to add to it." My "son" and I prayed, and as we did, I got the strongest impression that the second idea was true. What I had written in the chapters was enough, but that He wanted me to listen to Him and write what, I believe, He was saying in this Afterword. I have sat with Him, asking Him to remove anything that would hinder or distort His words from being true and accurate. Here is what I wrote down as I heard from Him:

> **"The readers of your book should not look for any easy formulas. Wisdom is gained by life. Living before Me and with Me will bring opportunities, each day, to exercise one or more of these aspects of wisdom. Those who know Me, My Son, and My Spirit, know We can have Our mind on a variety of topics, people, you, and what is going on at the times in which you are living. Seek Me in all things. I have things to tell you. You can—as I told you, John, many years ago—ask Me about everything! Wisdom is knowing My**

mind. Wisdom is being acquainted with My will, My words, My works, and, most of all, My ways. If you are progressively experiencing— did you get that?— EXPERIENCING and not just "knowing" these, then you will have entered Wisdom's house and dined at her table."

So be it, Lord!

ABOUT THE AUTHOR

John W. Wallace, a retired dentist, also pastored churches for 30 years. A speaker, trainer, author, advisor, and spiritual father to many, John now facilitates a network of pastors and leaders—Kingdom Culture Network. These relationships are built to encourage and support the advancement of the Kingdom of God and stimulate Kingdom living in and through God's leaders in their sphere of influence. John and his wife Suzanne have three children: Jason (wife Alison), Brennan (wife Lisa), and Lindsey (husband Chris). John and Suzanne dote over eight grandchildren.

kingdomnow4u@gmail.com

Made in the USA
Middletown, DE
03 October 2022